BATTLE OF NEW ORLEANS

A BRIEF HISTORY FROM BEGINNING TO END

HISTORY HUB

Bonus Downloads

*Get Free Books with **<u>Any Purchase</u>** History Shorts*

Every purchase comes with a FREE download!

Battle of New Orleans

A Brief History from Beginning to the End

History Shorts

CONTENTS

Chapter One
Introduction

The Battle of New Orleans, the lauded "end" of the War of 1812, was the final armed entanglement between the United States of America and Great Britain, fought on January 8, 1815. The Treaty of Ghent, which was signed in December 1814 and allowed the United States to join the Union, was the actual end of the War of 1812, but the opposing forces that marched on New Orleans as a means to secure Louisiana were oblivious to this.

In our discussion today, we are going to look at all of the numerous factors, big and small, that played a role in the glorious victory at The Battle of New Orleans. We will take an in-depth look at the trade restrictions that forced the United States of America to join the fray between Great Britain and France. Our research shows us that the still-developing America was keen to retain its new and hard-won independence from its former colonizer Great Britain, whilst being wary of the French ruler Napoleon. We will look at the internal conflicts America faced at the time, including political betrayals, uprisings from the indigenous people, and the unlikely partnerships they had to form to emerge victorious.

The Battle of New Orleans hinged on the strategic leadership of the up-and-coming General Andrew Jackson. In our discussion, we will look at the life events that shaped the young general. We will review the hardships and losses he suffered at the hands of the British government, which made him so determined to win the battle. We will also look at his contrasting beliefs and values, which made him hunt and persecute the Native American population whilst also adopting two of their own boys as his sons.

From our historical observing points of both the War of 1812 and the Battle of New Orleans, we will look at what led to the downfall of the British army and government. We'll examine whether it was just a lack of insight, resources, and planning that determined the outcome of both armed engagements or a case of wills prevailing.

Finally, we'll do an inventory of the aftermath of the Battle of New Orleans. We'll see that not all spoils of war were for the better of the collective people. America regained its sense of national pride and second independence, while Great Britain lost a huge colony once again. But it was the Native Americans who suffered the most. Left defenseless after the Battle of New Orleans and with General Andrew Jackson now in the White House, the fate of the indigenous people was sealed. Their forced removal from their ancestral land and the destruction of their culture and way of life still have ramifications centuries later.

Finally, we'll ask some pertinent questions about the legacy of the Battle of New Orleans and look at how it has impacted the freedoms and liberties the American people enjoy today. This fateful day in American history deserves all of the honor and glory it retains. It is up to us to continue to honor and remember the lives lost.

Chapter Two
The Origin

The War of 1812

To understand the magnitude of the victory won at the Battle of New Orleans and the impact it would have on the democracy of the United States of America, we have to go back to the beginning of the strife between the United States and Britain. This began with the War of 1812—the main source of animosity lay in the Americans resisting the British people's support of Native Americans standing against the United States' colonial settlement in the Northwest Territory.

Having so recently won their independence from Britain in 1783, the young United States of America was far from ready to give up their hard-won freedom, much less conceding their new land to the Native Americans once again. With Britain and France already fighting about which nation would have world dominance, Americans were not about to lay down and submit again.

The nation that held the oceans held the most political sway. The fledgling United States of America took umbrage to the British Naval Army encroaching on their maritime rights and cutting into their growing trade during the Napoleonic Wars. Motivated by their need to keep their freedom, the young republic declared war on Britain on June 18, 1812. The two main causes of the conflict were the British Orders-in-Council which limited America's trade with Europe, and the nasty habit the British Naval Army had of filling out their ship crews with seamen they stole from American merchant ships. It was rumored that up to 9000 Americans had been involuntarily drafted to the British fleets between 1803 and 1812.

At first glance, a war between the United States of America and Great Britain looked insurmountable. With just sixteen warships to their name, the Americans stood no chance against the 500-strong fleet held by the British. Taking the old adage that the best way to eat an elephant is to take small bites, the Americans, led by President James Madison, intended to invade Canada, a British colony, instead and hoped to use it as a bargaining chip in their negotiations about their maritime issues. The US army thought they would be viewed as liberators of freedom to the Canadians and have an easier victory as their numbers outmatched Canada's, but they underestimated the countrymen's loyalty to their homeland. The Canadian people banded together with the indigenous people of Northern America and forcefully put down all three of the American campaigns.

The US Army had not reckoned on the fact that the opposing army was led by a capable and ruthless leader, the esteemed Sir Isaac Brock, who headed up the Upper Canada (now Ontario) division. Leading his men into battle on August 16, 1812, Brock chased the US military force led by William Hull into an embarrassing defeat across the Canadian border. Hull was forced into surrendering Detroit without any shots fired. A relatively unknown fact, and one that even President Madison had neglected to take into account, was that the US army consisted of 7000 untrained, selfish in what they wanted from the battle, and poorly led by their commanding officer.

Detroit wouldn't be held by the British forces for long, as a battle in 1813 would see it retaken by the Americans again, but in 1812, victory remained sweet for the opposition. In successfully defending its North American colonies, the British gained back some of its respectability after fighting a war of life and death against Napoleon in Europe. This war set

America onto the world's stage, bringing its people's unbreakable spirit and industrious nature to the fore.

It may be called the War of 1812, but it, in fact, spanned over three years, well into 1815. The war was largely concluded simply because, after twenty years of fighting the French, Great Britain was tired of making sacrifices and enduring the massive expenses a war demanded of them. The bloodshed and devastation it caused eventually peaked, and a peace treaty was brokered that lasted more than two centuries. These days, the United States and the United Kingdom are peaceful allies, working together for the sake of world peace and prosperity for both countries.

The same cannot be said of the Native American community. Without the British army's support, these indigenous people found themselves at the mercy of the Americans. Their lands were taken, their people were indisposed, and they were left with huge cultural, infrastructural, and emotional damage. The Native Americans are nothing if not resilient, and even in the midst of all of the fallout, they found heroes to elevate, historic places to honor, and allegiances to maintain.

All of the damage caused could have been avoided if a simple misunderstanding had been cleared up from the beginning.

Chapter Three
The Misunderstanding

On December 24, 1814, a peace treaty, known as The Treaty of Ghent, was brokered between the United States of America and Great Britain. The Duke of Wellington and the Prime Minister of Great Britain were satisfied to agree to the treaty without demands for territory. The Americans, for their part, were eager to sign the treaty to avoid racking up even more foreign debt than they already had. Both parties thus agreed to the status quo ante bellum agreement, which saw each party's borders restored to what they had been before the war.

This misunderstanding arose because, while The Treaty of Ghent was signed in 1814, it was not ratified until February 17, 1815. Word of the treaty had not reached the British forces battling the Gulf coast at the time, and it certainly was too late to halt the advancement of a major attack. The British forces hoped that by taking the city, they could separate Louisiana from the rest of the United States of America. New Orleans was an attractive conquest prospect for Great Britain because it was one of the United States' critical trading ports. It is from this important port that

North America was able to ship its inland produce to South America, the Caribbean, and Europe. Slaves were sold in their thousands via this port. Capturing the New Orleans port meant cutting off the American trade chain and securing a port through which the British could reinforce their armies without being a risk. At the helm of this audacious battle plan for the British were Sir Alexander Cochrane, who led the Navy, and General Edward Pakenham, who commanded the boots on the ground. Their foe was the soon-to-be-hero General Andrew Jackson and his odd assortment of fighting-fit men: vagabonds, pirates, freed black men, and more. None of them were particularly well trained.

New Orleans, as America's wealthiest and third largest city at the time, would have found itself buckling under the violent British attack but for the timely warning that pirate Jean Lafitte gave to the Americans. The enemy of my enemy is my friend is the phrase that comes to mind here. Lafitte wisely bargained for a pardon of his and his men's crimes in exchange for helping the US forces to fight against the British army.

Under the strong leadership of General Andrew Johnson, the unlikely band of Americans held their own with just 4,500 troops. Having learned their lessons from the War of 1812, the US military forces were padded with expert marksmen who hailed from Kentucky and Tennessee. When faced with the British army's impressive 7,500 forces, the courageous US military was not cowed and did not hide. They rose admirably to the occasion and did not allow the imposing British military to penetrate their defenses. The measly US army defeated the British forces and forced them to retreat within 30 minutes. The Battle of New Orleans lasted little more than two hours.

The brutal losses at the end of the Battle of New Orleans speak volumes about how the entanglement unfolded: British leader General Pakenham succumbed to battle injuries while 2000 of his soldiers were injured, wounded, or killed. In stark contrast, the much smaller US army had only eight fallen soldiers and thirteen injured men. None was as surprised by their victory as the American army men themselves.

The Battle of Orleans was but a small blip in the overall landscape of the war, but it is revered as the fight that restored the American patriotic dream and as the last armed engagement between the United States of America and Great Britain. It also helped to make America a global force to be reckoned with. The surprising victory was led by the formidable General Andrew Jackson. This victory forced the British to formally recognize the United States of America's claim to Louisiana and West Florida. Additionally, Louisiana was formally introduced into the Union.

History marks the Battle of New Orleans as the deciding factor in the victory of the United States of America over Great Britain, but that honor actually belongs to the Treaty of Ghent. The irony is that a battle that took place after peace was brokered remains so iconic in American history. January 8 would be celebrated with major celebrations for the next fifty years, honoring the brave Americans who fought so valiantly and the war hero who led them to this significant victory.

One fact that remains undisputed is that General Andrew Jackson arose from the Battle of New Orleans as a war hero.

Chapter Four
Andrew Jackson, future president, and war hero

From the bloody battlefield of the Battle of New Orleans, an unlikely war hero emerged: the esteemed General Andrew Jackson. "Andy," as he was informally known, had led a small and poorly armed troop against the mighty force of the British Army and had prevailed against all odds. In an armed engagement that was deemed unnecessary since the Treaty of Ghent was already in effect, Jackson still proved his mettle, and this unexpected victory would set him on the path to the White House.

The future war hero and president was born on March 15, 1767, in the Waxhaw Settlement of North California. His parents, Andrew Jackson Sr and Elizabeth Hutchinson, were Scottish-Irish colonists. A religious couple following the Presbyterian faith, the Jackson emigrated from Ulster, Ireland, in 1765.The youngest of three sons, Jackson did not get to meet his father, who died in a logging accident three weeks before his birth. Elizabeth, perhaps realizing her son had a special talent for learning, planned to have him educated as a minister. She paid for him to be taught by a local clergyman. Jackson learned to speak, read and write as well as received lessons in Greek and Latin. His fiery temper, though, made him unsuitable for the ministry, and he enlisted in military service alongside his two older brothers, Hugh and Robert instead.

As a man in service, Jackson racked up a series of incredible achievements quite quickly, including eventually becoming Attorney General of Nashville in 1791. Serving as a courier and scout, the young soldier participated in the Battle of Hanging Rock on August 6, 1780. Following a string of unfortunate events which led to the deaths of his brothers and mother, a stint of being held captive, and contracting smallpox, Jackson was left as an orphan at age 14 and with a deep hatred of all things British. He especially abhorred the British's emphasis on aristocracy and political privilege.

By the time the Battle of New Orleans rolled around, Andrew Jackson was a revered and feared general. In 1813, after America had been repeatedly defeated by the British, Jackson was finally called upon to take action. He raised an army of over 2000 men to march on New Orleans. After some confusion and a refusal to back down later, Jackson spent 1814 reigning terror on indigenous people and claiming new territories for the United States.

Upon his arrival in New Orleans on December 1, 1814. Worried about the loyalty of the Creole and Spanish residents to their British overlords, Jackson implemented martial law on the inhabitants of the city. Pooling his resources with the pirate Jean Lafitte and recruiting freed slaves to his cause, the General formed a 5000-man strong army to defend New Orleans against the incoming British forces.

Using his many years of military experience, Jackson built a fortified position for his army. This strategic decision was one of the deciding factors that helped the US army defeat the British forces on January 8, 1815. While the British attempted a full-frontal assault, Jackson's men were able to easily target their foes and remain safe behind their parapets. The battle, which lasted less than two hours and in which it was clear the Americans had the winning hand within 30 minutes, was a bloody affair.

The Americans suffered a mere 60 casualties compared to the British army's 2000 losses, including that of their leader General Packenham. Had Jackson not chosen to further risk the ire of the public by ordering executions of deserters and the eviction of French residents, his reputation might not have been as tarnished as it was. It likely did not make any difference to the man himself, who emerged as a war hero from the Battle of New Orleans.

This victory ensured America's control of the region between New Orleans and Mobile. He was awarded a Congressional Gold Medal for his heroic efforts, and this achievement stood him in good stead when he decided to run for the presidential office. Andrew Jackson was inaugurated as the President of the United States of America on March 4, 1929. He served as president for two terms.

General Andrew Jackson's tenacity and grit, learned from a hard childhood and a long life in service to his home country, made him a hero more than any war could. Yet, history continues to remember him as the man and general who helped to ensure America's hard-earned and well-deserved freedom.

Chapter Five

The Rise of the United States of America in the War of 1812

Americans are known for their indomitable spirit, and for many, this can be traced back to the War of 1812. Despite being defeated over and over again by the invading British army, the American forces kept fighting back and eventually emerged victorious. But where did this patriotic spirit come from, and how did it rise?

As the 19th century dawned, the United States of America found itself at the center of a war it did not ask for nor did it actively want to participate in. Unfortunately, staying out of the horrifying war between Great Britain and France under the contentious Napoleon Bonaparte was unavoidable since the two warring factions tried to prevent the US from trading with each other.

The relatively young American government, having just achieved its independence from Britain, was not partial to having its shipping ports restrained. The lawmakers attempted to remove themselves from the British-French conflict by passing and implementing the Non-Intercourse

Act in 1809. Under this act, America was strictly prohibited from trading with either Britain or France. While the Non-Intercourse Act proved to be ineffective, it does show that the United States of America was rising to meet more powerful players on the global stage. The seeds of national pride were already being planted.

In May 1810, the Non-Intercourse Act was abolished, and the powers that be passed a bill stating that if either Great Britain or France dropped trade relations with the United States of America, the country would implement the Non-Disclosure Act with the opposition.

Napoleon seduced the United States government with hints of dropping France's trading restrictions, and the US President at the time, James Madison, blocked all trade with Great Britain. Adding to Great Britain's woes with the United States were several new Congressmen, chiefly Henry Clay and John C.Calhoun, who were chafing under the British's violations of their maritime rights and were itching for war.

The War of 1812 was a heated and bloody result of both the victory of the Battle of Tippecanoe in 1811 and President Madison feeling the pressure of his congressman. President Madison finally rose to the occasion and signed a declaration of war against Britain. The House and Senate were not of one mind when the bill was passed, but the War of 1812 went ahead. We now know that the war ultimately did not go as smoothly as the US government thought it would, but it did give rise to nationalism, pride, and inherent faith in the American dream. A dream that soon many more immigrants to this great country would follow and one that would inspire countless novels, artwork, movies, and songs. The War of 1812 would see the rise of many war heroes who played even bigger roles in the rise of the United States of America.

Hailed as the "second war of independence," the War of 1812 instilled a sense of national pride in Americans that is hard to defeat to this day!

Chapter Six
The Rise of the Battle of New Orleans

The iconic Battle of New Orleans lives large as a military and patriotic legend in the minds of Americans and the history books. If not for the detailed accounts kept, letters saved, and military strategies recorded, it would be utterly impossible to believe that 2000 Americans, an untrained group of soldiers, pirates, indigenous people, and former slaves, stood victorious against Great Britain's formidable military force. But what gave rise to this legend?

From what we've discussed before, we know that gave rise to the Battle of New Orleans was General Andrew Jackson's unwillingness to stick to the rules of engagement, the unbelievable and terribly unfortunate late arrival of the news of the Treaty of Ghent, and each of the opposing sides being tired of fighting. That Battle of New Orleans was the final showdown for the warring countries, and both were determined to win, no matter the cost.

One way or another, a country was going to emerge victorious - it was just the United States of America's destiny to be the victor. What Andrew

Jackson knew, perhaps better than his foes, was that bringing different men together for a common cause was better than having them divided and fighting each other. His unusual armed forces were made up of a disparaging group of men, and their unique talents, along with a strategic battleground position, ensured they caused considerable damage to the British army.

The Battle of New Orleans, whilst celebrated for the victory of the day on January 8, 1815, was actually a series of smaller skirmishes that ran from December 1814 to January 1815.The outcome of the final battle was as much about the American army's defense plan as it was about the British forces' poor planning. Great Britain's General and company severely underestimated the crafty General Andrew Jackson's troops of unusual soldiers. Underestimating the strength and wit of the indigenous people, pirates, and former slaves, as well as their belief in following General Andrew Jackson's lead, cost General Pakenham and his advisors sorely.

It's unclear what the beleaguered British government would have done with Louisiana if they had won The Battle of New Orleans. Some speculate that they would have given the land to the indigenous people as an independent country to counteract the escalating tensions between the United States of America and British-owned North America.Perhaps they would have ceded the land back to Spain. What is clear is that either way, the indigenous people were the ultimate losers of this war.

Luckily for modern Americans, the US army held its own and rose to defend their young country. The Battle of New Orleans has risen to become the most well-remembered and most revered act of armed engagement in American history, with monuments constructed in its honor, books written to analyze the battle strategies used by the United States of America and Great Britain, and historians writing numerous papers about it. The peace brokered by this important battle has ensured more than two centuries of good relations between the formerly warring nations.

Are You Enjoying Reading?

As an independent publisher

with a tiny marketing budget

we rely on readers, like you.

If you're receiving help from this book,

would you please take a moment to write a brief review?

We really appreciate it.

Chapter Seven
The Rise of General Andrew Jackson

When looking back at the incredible life and career of General Andrew Jackson, it is easy to see where the future President's rise began. Yes, The Battle of New Orleans is seen as the beginning of his meteoric rise to greatness, but the fact is that the seeds of greatness were planted long before, in his difficult childhood and early days of military service.

The father of the modern Democratic Party was a Revolutionary War prisoner of war. He and his family were taken by the British, and that horrifying experience gave rise to Jackson's disdain for Great Britain's practices. Jackson's face and hands were scarred by a soldier during his imprisonment. Jackson's offense? Not shining the officer's boots when he was ordered to do so.

The future President's imprisonment made him determined to make something of himself. He taught himself to be a frontier lawyer. He passed the bar when he was twenty years old and was appointed solicitor of the western district of North Carolina. His great ambition saw him ruling as a Tennessee Supreme Court judge until 1804. This was a remarkable achievement for a young man who had flunked out as an aspiring man of the cloth and lost his entire family to an unnecessary war.

Returning to his love for the military, Jackson won the 1802 election to become the leader of the Tennessee militia. So great was his prowess at the Battle of Horseshoe Bend in 1814 that Jackson was awarded the command of the army that defeated the British forces at the Battle of New Orleans.

Jackson was a man of many contradictions. He fought the Native American people in numerous battles, evicted and had them relocated during his presidential terms, and contributed to much of their historical inaccuracies, but he was also the adoptive father of two Native American boys. Through his children, he was friendly with several Native Americans.

He was known for his fiery temperament, which made him unsuitable for the life of a minister that his mother hoped he would be. That same temper gave him the drive to win his military and presidential campaigns. While General Pakenham's orders were to march on New Orleans no matter what news he received about The Treaty of Ghent, General

Jackson's decision to engage in battle was out of sheer impatience and the desire to win.

Allying himself with former enemies to take down a bigger one was a smart move on his part. It showed he had grit, a mind of his own, and the courage to see his daring plan through to its bloody climax. His victory at the Battle of New Orleans was not just the rise of his own political career but also the rise of the United States of America as a global political force that was to be reckoned with.

What goes up must come down, though, and the fall of both the United States of America and General Andrew Jackson would be a swift one.

Chapter Eight
The Fall of the War of 1812

The young United States of America's independence was unfortunately threatened as the fledgling country found itself at the center of the strife between the warring nations of Great Britain and France. America's trading ports were being targeted to prevent either of the warring factions from trading with them. Great Britain, specifically, was pilfering able-bodied American men from the US's vessels and enslaving them on their own ships.

For three years, the British used brute force to take back what they deemed "their" land in America but lacked the strategy to fully enforce their ill-begotten gains and use it to their advantage. Furthermore, they were trying to conquer the land they were not familiar with and failing to deliver on promises to the indigenous people who were relying on them for help.

By the time the Treaty of Ghent was signed in 1814, both countries were just so tired of fighting all of the time, losing countless men and becoming bankrupt due to the cost of war. The United States of America's President

James Madison, seduced by Napoleon's trade agreement concessions, declared war on Great Britain for not sticking to the law of the Non-Intercourse Act in 1811 and thus began the War of 1812.

What seems to be at the heart of the Fall of the War of 1812 is a discourse, not just between the warring countries but within each of their ranks too. President Madison received great backlash from his Secretary of State Robert Smith, who stated his pro-British sympathies to the British Prime Minister. Smith, instead of quietly accepting his punishment and becoming the US's ambassador to Russia, leaked cabinet papers as part of a smear campaign against the President. Smith resigned in April 1811, and President Madison went ahead with his declaration of war against the British.

The British, eager to put down this war campaign so that they could go back to fighting the French, held their own in their colony of Canada and won several skirmishes because the Americans' attacks were clumsy and uncoordinated. The British even managed to burn the United States capital, Washington, to the ground in August of 1814. What they didn't account for is the rise of General Andrew Jackson and his determination to remove the British scourge from his homeland.

Helping to win a few of the smaller battles in the War of 1812 helped General Andrew Jackson show off his strategic mind and battle prowess and impress the powers that be so much that he was eventually given command of the army that would protect Louisiana. While the Treaty of Ghent was signed in December 1814, it was not ratified until February 1815. While the hard-fought and hard-won War of 1812 fell, Jackson and the Battle of New Orleans' stars were about to rise into the world's historical archives and the White House. General Jackson became President Andrew Jackson thirteen years after his resounding victory at the much-revered Battle of New Orleans.

Chapter Nine

The Fall of the British at the Battle of New Orleans

For the advancing British army, led by General Pakenham, successfully defeated the small ragtag United States of America military forces, led by an enterprising General Andrew Jackson in New Orleans, appeared to be an easy slam dunk. History books now reveal that General Pakenham's greatest folly was underestimating his opponent and being far too cocksure about a resounding victory.

The fall of the British army can be traced to their overconfidence, as a result of having just been victorious at the Battle of Lake Borgne in early December 1814. With the smell of smoke and ash still heavy in the air following the British military setting fire to the United States of America's capital, Washington DC, General Pakenham was eager to continue his winning streak. With strict orders from his superiors to continue his march on Louisiana no matter the outcome of the War of 1812, General Pakenham set about advancing on New Orleans.

Had General Pakenham scrutinized his alleged allies a bit more closely, he would have realized sooner that trusting the known smuggler and pirate Jean Lafitte was a very bad idea. Lafitte, always out for more gold and glory, has turned his coat and deflected to the United States of America's army, warning General Andrew Jackson about the impending British attack and how best to counteract it.

General Pakenham did not take into account that as much as General Jackson was despised by the local indigenous people, mutual enemies could be banded together to fight for a common cause. In this case, it was national patriotism and the desire to keep their young country free from the overbearing Great Britain. General Pakenham may have thought that General Jackson's untrained company of vagabonds, pirates, former slaves, and indigenous people would cower in the face of his 10 000 strong forces, but they did not.

General Andrew Jackson smartly used his unlikely company's in-depth knowledge of their homeland as well as an advantageous fort on the Left Bank to stave off a poorly planned full frontal assault by General Pakenham and his forces. It was a David vs. Goliath battle of Biblical proportions, and in the end, the Americans emerged as the victor.

General Pakenham, his second-in-command, and more than 2000 of their men fell to the onslaught of General Andrew Jackson and his motley crew. The British tried and failed to launch a follow-up attack after the Battle of New Orleans. They abandoned their armed entanglement efforts when the Treaty of Ghent was ratified, and the United States of America was accepted into the Union.

The Battle of New Orleans remains one of America's greatest victories and the dawn of its second independence. For Great Britain, that fateful battle marked the beginning of the end of its holdfast on one of its former colonies. Peace reigned between the two countries for decades until the American Civil War. History was doomed to repeat itself, and the United States of America remains the Land of the Free to this day.

Chapter Ten
The Aftermath of the Battle of New Orleans

General Andrew Jackson's unlikely troops' resounding victory on the battlefield, as well as Napoleon's timely fall, ensured that Louisiana was now firmly the United States of America's land. Great Britain and Spain were forced to accept this.

This victory was a second declaration of independence for the United States of America and renewed a great sense of national pride in their young country. It also ensured that the United States of America formed part of the Union. The Americans enjoyed a massive expansion of their territories and established their military. The battle gave rise to many expressions and symbols that now form a huge part of the modern American resident's identity.

The Eighth of January became a national holiday that was celebrated with great fanfare from 1828 to 1861. It was as important a celebration as the Fourth of July. The United States of America remained unified for the next 45 years until the American Civil War.

For Great Britain, their loss at the Battle of New Orleans signified the start of their war woes all over again. Napoleon escaped from Elba on February 26 and wasted no time taking back his power in France. This, in turn, led him to renew his war with Great Britain and greater Europe.

For the Native Americans, the Battle of New Orleans and the Americans' victory was a devastating blow. Dispossessed of their land and political autonomy, the indigenous tribes were forced from their homes. After already losing nearly 15% of the Creek population and twenty-three million acres of land in the Battle of Horseshoe Bend in March 1814, the Native American community was not prepared for the aftermath of the Battle of New Orleans.

The indigenous people lost their chief Tecumseh as well as the protection of Great Britain in the Battle of New Orleans. While General Andrew Jackson was hailed as a war hero and eventually was elected as President of the United States of America, he continued to wage his war on the Native Americans. In 1830, he signed the Indian Removal Act, further displacing the indigenous tribes, destroying their lives, and ruining their way of life. An estimated 46 000 Native Americans were forced to relocate to "Indian Territory," which is what is now known as

Oklahoma. More than 4000 of the people died of starvation, exposure to the elements, and disease on their journey to their new land.

General and later President Andrew Jackson's drive for political power devastated thousands of indigenous families, their tribes, their lifestyle, and their history. While reparations have since been made and continue to be made, history must never forget that American pride is built on the suffering of a once-thriving community. These people are now relegated to reservations, and their integral part in history is often overlooked or downplayed.

The Battle of New Orleans remains a fixture and icon of patriotism for Americans and an example of when Great Britain was defeated by a small army in the Land of the Free.

Chapter Eleven
Conclusion

"The sons of America have given new proof how impossible it is to conquer freemen fighting in defense of all that is dear to them. Henceforward we shall be respected by nations who, mistaking our character, had treated us with the utmost contempt and outrage. Years will continue to develop our inherent qualities, until, from being the youngest and the weakest, we shall become the most powerful nation in the universe." — General Andrew Jackson, after the Battle of New Orleans

The key takeaway lesson we can take from The Battle of New Orleans is this: we are stronger together than when we are divided. It is perhaps a lesson we, as modern Americans, should bear in mind, as our nation is currently divided by politics, religious beliefs, racism, and gender inequality.

General Andrew Jackson and his band of misfit military men gave the young United States of America something to fight for and a renewed sense of national pride. By bringing together such a disparate group of soldiers, pirates, former slaves, and endangered indigenous folk, Jackson set out to prove that the love for one country and the right to protect their homeland was more important than the color of their skin, their differences in religious beliefs and their desire to break down societal conventions.

Another key lesson to learn here is that men will follow where great pioneers lead. The British army fell to an American one that was finally led by a powerful man who believed in the strength of his convictions and what his people were capable of doing. Jackson's strategic mind, his knowledge of the law, and his hatred for the British spurred him onto greatness and to think outside of the box when conventional battle strategies and reinforcements were found lacking.

The Eighth of January became an honored celebration for decades after the Battle of New Orleans. Andrew Jackson became one of the United States of America's most well-known presidents. Honors won on that battlefield are still remembered today as a sense of national pride remains. Our blood runs blue, red, and white. For America!

Chapter Twelve
Discussion Question

Colonization is one of the defining features of Great Britain's history. The United States of America fought hard to win its independence from Britain. Expanding on their Northern American Territory, they were colonizing the indigenous people's land. How did that make them any different from Great Britain?

Discussion Question

Reparation is an ongoing process that must be managed carefully. While the United States of America has been slowly making theirs to the indigenous people, can the same be said of Great Britain? To what extent should the British be making reparations to the Native American communities?

Discussion Question

Communication networks were rudimentary at best in 1814/1815. Is there any possible way that the Battle of New Orleans could have been prevented? While it did not change the landscape of the war completely, do you think it was a necessary event?

Discussion Question

War makes for strange bedfellows. General Andrew Jackson rounded up an assortment of strange characters for his army, including pirates, free black men, and others for The Battle of New Orleans. Somehow, they emerged victorious. Do you think the outcome would have been different if Jackson had had better-trained men?

Discussion Question

General Andrew Jackson held a particular bitterness for the British after all of the losses he suffered at their hands. Do you think his determination to win the Battle of New Orleans was more revenge-driven than an act of patriotism? Should he have recused himself from this particular battle?

Discussion Question

The United States of America became embroiled in the war between Great Britain and France through no real fault of their own. What do you imagine might have happened to the country if they had not chosen to start The War of 1812? What would the state of the world look like now??

Discussion Question

The Battle of New Orleans was fought over a few months, with January 8, 1815, being the day of victory for the Americans. If modern journalists were covering this battle today, what do you think their reports would be like? How could we compare the Battle of New Orleans to the current war between Ukraine and Russia?

Discussion Question

The Eight of January is no longer celebrated as a national holiday. Do you think this is fair? Should the lives lost at the Battle of New Orleans not be honored in some way?

Chapter Thirteen
Quiz Question

1. **True/False:** Morale ebbed and flowed during the War of 1812. Many of the untrained soldiers were tradesmen of different occupations. One of them, Francis Scott Key, was industrious enough during this time to pen the American National Anthem.

2. **True/False:** History makes the Battle of New Orleans the deciding victory and end of the War of 1812. If news of The Treaty of Ghent had reached the British Army in time, the Battle of New Orleans would never have happened. America would have been on the road to independence sooner.

3. **True/False:** General Andrew Jackson served as President of the United States of America for two terms. In the aftermath of the Battle of New Orleans, his reputation was tarnished quite a bit. His victory at the Battle of New Orleans has been overlooked in history.

4. **True/False:** The United States of America engaged in war with Great Britain after Napoleon led them to believe he would drop France's trade restrictions with their country. If France had not offered that proposal, America would have continued to trade with Britain. The War of 1812 would have been avoided altogether.

5. **True/ False:** General Andrew Jackson formed his winning army at the Battle of New Orleans from a group of pirates, former slaves, and indigenous people. He tried getting additional military support, but the US troops were severely understaffed due to the War of 1812. The unique skills of his unusual troops helped him to win the battle.

6. **True/False:** General Andrew Jackson had no great love for the Native Americans. He passed the Indian Removal Act in 1830, which displaced thousands of their people. He did, however, adopt two of them as his sons..

7. **True/False:** The aftermath of the Battle of New Orleans had a great positive impact on everyone involved. The Americans have a restored sense of nationalism. The British retreated to a peaceful life at home. The Native Americans were left to live as they had before.

8. **True/ False:** The British Army was led by General Pakenham and his mighty military force. They were trained well. They did not underestimate their opponents and won the Battle of New Orleans.

Quiz Answer

1. True

2. True.

3. False: His victory at the Battle of New Orleans made General Andrew Jackson a war hero. It raised him in the esteem of the American people.

4. False: The United States of America was already at odds with Great Britain because the latter was opposing their expansion into Northern America. Britain was providing aid to the Native American tribes.

5. True.

6. True

7. False: The British were re-engaged in war with the French. The Native Americans were forcibly removed from their lands.

8. False: he British army, while well-trained, grossly underestimated the United States forces. They were thoroughly defeated at the Battle of New Orleans..

Bibliography

Chapter 2: The War of 1812, "War of 1812: New Orleans [Image 4 of 32]" by DVIDSHUB is licensed under CC BY 2.0. To view a copy of this license, visit https://creativecommons.org/licenses/by/2.0/?ref=openverse.

Chapter 3: General Andrew Jackson, the future President of the United States of America, is honored with a statue. The General led an unlikely armed force to victory against the British in 1815.

Chapter 5: The rise of the Battle of New Orleans. General Andrew Jackson put together a ragtag army of soldiers, pirates, former slaves and more to fight at The Battle of New Orleans. This unlikely army won the battle.

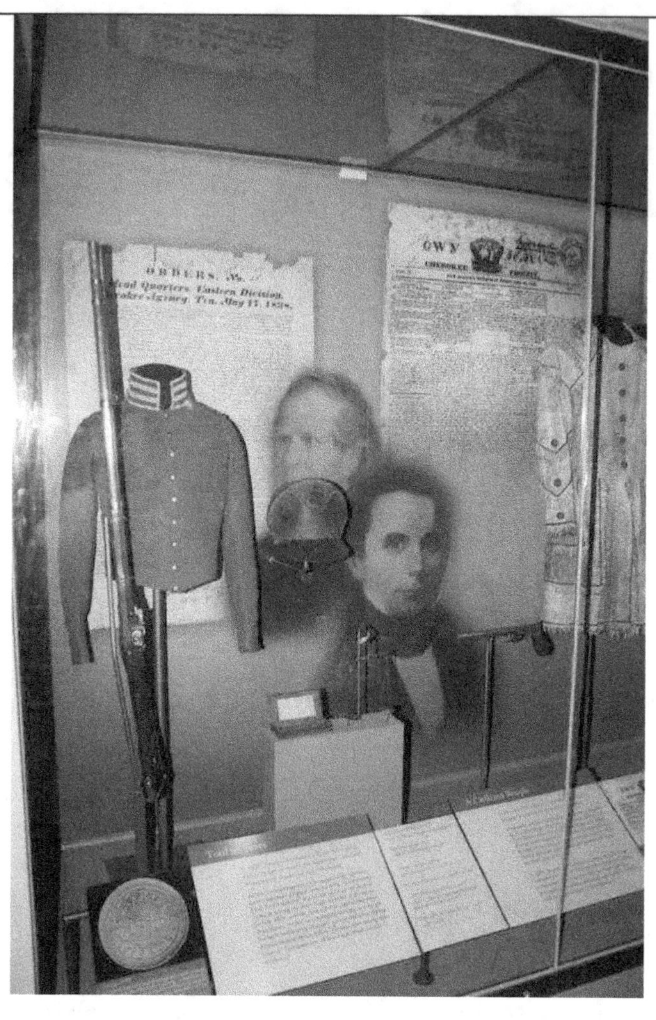

Chapter 7: The Native Americans were hardest hit by the Indian Removal Act, in the aftermath of the Battle of New Orleans. The ramifications of this Act exist today. The Aftermath: "Trail of Tears, Expulsion of Southeast Indian Nations by U.S. Army and Popular Democracy, 1830s" by Gary Lee Todd, Ph.D. is marked with CC0 1.0. To view the terms, visit https://creativecommons.org/publicdomain/zero/1.0/?ref=openverse

.

Bonus Downloads

*Get Free Books with **Any Purchase** History Shorts*

Every purchase comes with a FREE download!

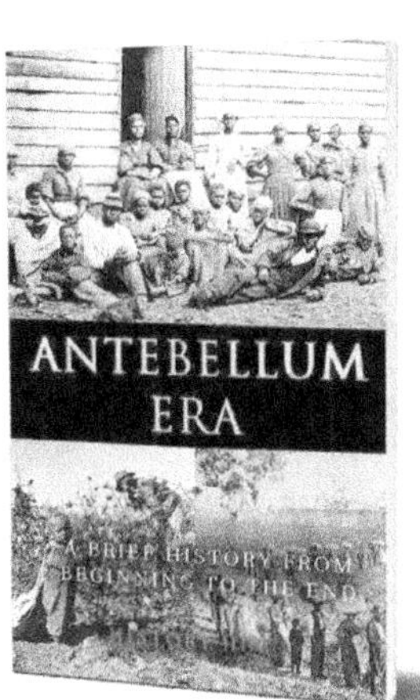

Thank You For Reading

As an independent publisher

with a tiny marketing budget

we rely on readers, like you.

If you're receiving help from this book,

would you please take a moment to write a brief review?

We really appreciate it.